WHAT NAILS IT

WHAT NAILS IT

GREIL MARCUS

THE 2023 WINDHAM-CAMPBELL LECTURE

YALE UNIVERSITY PRESS
NEW HAVEN AND LONDON

The *Why I Write* series is published
with assistance from the Windham-
Campbell Literature Prizes, which are
administered by the Beinecke Rare
Book and Manuscript Library at
Yale University.

Yale University Press books may be
purchased in quantity for educational,
business, or promotional use.
For information, please e-mail
sales.press@yale.edu (U.S. office) or
sales@yaleup.co.uk (U.K. office).

Set in Yale and News Gothic BT type.
Printed in the United States of America.

Library of Congress Control
Number: 2023952231
ISBN 978-0-300-27245-1
(hardcover : alk. paper)

A catalogue record for this book is
available from the British Library.

This paper meets the requirements
of ANSI/NISO Z39.48-1992
(Permanence of Paper).

10 9 8 7 6 5 4 3 2 1

To Jenny, Cecily, and Paula
For the spring and summer of 2022

In memory of Emily Marcus
December 10, 1969–January 31, 2023

CONTENTS

WHAT NAILS IT

1

Greil Gerstley

I write for fun. I write for play. I write for the play of words. I write to discover what I want to say and how to say it — and the nerve to say it.

The key word for me here is not fun, play — but discover. I live for those moments when something appears on the page as if of its own volition — as if I had nothing to do with what is now looking me in the face.

In 1965, Bob Dylan described his song "Like a Rolling Stone" as "twenty pages of vomit," boiled down to a point of hatred — well, he said later, maybe ten pages — but much later, almost fifty years later, he described it very differently. "It's like a ghost is writing a song like that," he said, talking to Robert Hilburn of the *Los Angeles Times*. "It gives you the song and then it goes away, it goes away. You don't know what it means. Except the ghost picked me to write the song."

That's a very evocative, very romantic account of what anyone who engages in any sort of creative activity experiences at any time. For a lot of people, that sense of an evanescent gift, the genie granting you a wish even if you never asked for it—that sense of visitation—is what it's all for: a moment of inexplicable clarity. "When you put the music with words and things together, the songs just make themselves," the 1950s New Orleans rock 'n' roll pianist and singer Huey "Piano" Smith once said; he wrote Frankie Ford's "Sea Cruise," he wrote "Don't You Just Know It," but he's best remembered for "The Rockin' Pneumonia and the Boogie-Woogie Flu"—a follow-up, "Tu-Ber-Cu-Lucas and the Sinus Blues," was not so hot. But he went on: "After you listen on it," he said of putting things together, "it says something of its own self, that you hadn't planned." Talking about stand-up comedy, Richard Belzer said the same thing. "The greatest thing for me," he said, "is when I make the audience laugh in a moment that could only happen that night with that audience"—when Bob Dylan recorded "Like a Rolling Stone," live in the studio with a six-piece band, over two days and twenty-four takes, twenty-four stabs, false starts, breakdowns, only twice did they make it all the way through the four-verse, six-minute song, and the second time was all trip, stumble, and fall. That's what Richard Belzer was talking about, that single moment when what you're writing, painting, singing, telling, speaks in its own voice, which is and isn't yours: "Sometimes I laugh with the audience because I'm hearing the joke the same time they are."

That feeling of no, I didn't think that, I didn't write that, *where did that come from?* — and I mean that literally, absolutely having no memory of creating, composing, fashioning, what is there staring at you, saying, *Alright, here it is, what are you going to make of this?* — I remember the first time it happened.

It was 1973. I had dropped out of graduate school at Berkeley after finishing my course work and barely passing my orals — I sat for three hours outside the room where I'd met with three professors, going through every stage of grief, denial, disbelief, fury, and finally not caring. Then I was offered the chance to teach the American Studies Honors Seminar — a two-semester, year-long course for sophomores, with one teacher each from History, English, and my department, Political Science. I was preening over the prestige: no graduate student had ever taught it. I had taken it over 1964 and 1965, with Michael Rogin from Political Science and Larzer Ziff from English. It was a revelation; it introduced me to the terrain, and the conversation, that for good or ill would lie behind what I would end up doing for the rest of my life. It was that classroom engagement, when an atmosphere is conjured up where anything can be said and anything can be understood, where any idea or any argument opens up instantly and naturally into another, until finally the whole class finds itself at the top of a pyramid, dizzy with the notion that now, with the day's class over, you have to find a way down, which is a version of that out-of-nowhere sentence showing up on a page and asking you if you can take the next step, or fail it, fail the dare it's throwing at you, abandon it as if was never there at all.

That's a translation of how the class actually worked. In the evening a number of us would gather in the seminar room, which was on an upper floor of the great main library, and which was also a library in itself, the books the class was made of — Perry Miller's biography of Jonathan Edwards, a battered but intact original edition of John Adams's *Discourses on Davila*. We'd stay, reading and talking, long after the library was locked up for the night, and at one or two in the morning climb out of a window on a rope, one by one. It fell to the last person out to show up the next morning when the library opened and pull up the rope.

Through most of graduate school I'd been writing for *Rolling Stone,* then *Creem*. Starting in 1968, I'd been sending in record reviews to *Rolling Stone;* they were printing them. It was a professional operation, at least compared to the so-called underground newspapers of the time. I was shocked after the first review ran to find a check for $12.50 in the mail a week later. A few months after that I met someone who worked for the paper—that's what it was called then, a fold-over newsprint tabloid—and started complaining about the record review section: it was all writing about lyrics, nobody was writing about music, nobody was writing about how anything felt, how anything moved, how anything moved you. A few days later I got a call from the editor, Jann Wenner, who I'd met when we were both freshmen at Cal, though this was five years later and we hadn't seen each other since. "This is Jann," he said, as if we'd been talking that day before and he was just picking up the conversation where it had left off. "If you think the records section is so terrible, why don't you edit it?" So I did, for six months, until after the murderous Rolling Stones show at Altamont at the tail end of 1969, the most violent day of my life, when I was burned out. I recruited the late Ed Ward to replace me, and I kept writing, until I was fired six months later. I went on to the much scruffier and much more try-anything *Creem* magazine, from Detroit—*Rolling Stone* in 1968 and 1969 was very try-anything, because there were no rules, except that we were making our own, and *Creem* wasn't making any rules at all.

Then in 1972 I left graduate school. I'd always assumed I'd become a professor. I had such great professors at Berkeley—along with Michael Rogin and Larzer Ziff, John Schaar and Norman Jacobson. They were inspiring figures. They were devoted to students. They looked you in the eye. They let you know that they believed you had something to contribute, in a class, in a paper, even to the field, the discipline, the discourse, the conversation that had been going on for centuries, and you felt called to try to live up to that. But as a teacher myself, I wasn't. I had no patience, and a teacher without patience is not a teacher. Instead of "Tell us what you mean" when a student said something that seemed wrong, I heard "How could you say that?"

coming out of my mouth. When I thought everyone was missing the point I'd pontificate for five minutes and shut everyone up for the rest of the class. When I taught again, after nearly thirty years of never stepping inside a classroom, I was ready to learn that if there was a point that absolutely needed to be made, an idea that simply had to be addressed, even a fact that needed to be stated, if I could keep quiet for five minutes, someone in the class would find their way there. I found out that the ideal class would be one in which I didn't say a word — once, at Princeton, it actually happened.

But at Berkeley I came home from every class angry and in despair. I had wonderful students, three of whom are close friends to this day. But I was cheating them out of their own education. I'd had enough bad teachers not to want to become one. I realized I couldn't spend the rest of my life doing something I didn't like and wasn't good at. At that point the other thing I knew how to do was write. So now, after four years as a journalist, I was trying to write a book.

It was a book that came straight out of that 1964–65 American Studies seminar, when I was nineteen, Michael Rogin was twenty-seven, and Larzer Ziff was thirty-seven. Out of that, and out of living my life to the Beatles, the Rolling Stones, Bob Dylan, rediscovering Little Richard and Elvis Presley, discovering Robert Johnson. Now, for what would in 1975 be called *Mystery Train: Images of America in Rock 'n' Roll Music,* I was writing about Sly and the Family Stone, within the frame of the black folklore figure Stagger Lee — the bad man, the man of impulse and appetite, a walking advertisement for freedom and revenge, style and death, living life without limits, someone who'd kill someone else over a hat. A real person, as it turned out, one "Stag" Lee Shelton, who in 1895 in St. Louis shot Billy Lyons in an argument over a Stetson hat in Bill Curtis's saloon — now it's an office building. Years later I was taken there; I took twigs from a bush in the landscaping.

Right off, maybe the next night, someone composed the street ballad "Stagolee and Billy." Within days it was traveling up and down the Mississippi. Within a decade or two, with the real facts behind the song forgotten or never known — never mattering: who cared where a song came from when the story it told was so good everyone wanted to claim it? — people would tell you they remembered Stagger Lee, heard about him, knew someone who knew him, in Chicago, Memphis, New Orleans, even New York. Lloyd Price, from Kenner, Louisiana, now home of the Louis Armstrong International Airport, remembered growing up and watching local pimps and gangsters with their colored zoot suits and Cadillacs: to young boys like him "they were all Stagger Lees." Stationed in Korea, he staged a play based on the old ballad. When he took his version of the song to the top of the charts in 1958, "Stagger Lee" was stomping through every town in the country; the whole nation sang the song.

Lee Shelton would have heard it himself, in dozens of versions, over the next decade after Billy Lyons was buried and into the decade after that, in and out of prison, until he died there in 1912. But as a song it was also a legend, a myth that from its start traveled through the next century and beyond, as music, in novels, in movies, by 2008 even a porn film, starring Sasha Gray and directed by one Benny Profane.

But all that history was written later. With no facts at hand, even after months of searching, it was the myth I was writing about. I was trying to imagine who Stagger Lee would be, how he would act, how the world would open up before him or close around him. He was a hero. He played out his string. Then it snapped back around his neck. I started with a declarative sentence.

After that, some uncanny cadence took over the words. As if in a trance, the words were making their own rhythm:

> Stagger Lee is a free man, because he takes
> chances and scoffs at the consequences.
> Others gather to fawn over him, until he
> shatters in a grimy celebration of needles,
> juice, and noise. Finally he is alone in a slow
> bacchanal, where his buddies, in a parody of
> friendship, devote themselves to a study of
> the precise moment of betrayal.

What came down, I think, what appeared, were those words "slow bacchanal." That was the prize, that was the treasure. I just had to figure out what to do with it, find out what it wanted, what images it was making, what the story was that was hidden in the two words.

So that's why I write: to reach the state where that can happen, and then to see if I can still find my way in and out of that cave. But of course there's more to it than that — or anyway another version of the same story.

Writing is not only an odd craft, a keeping company with ghosts giving you songs and visitations giving you words. People may say, to other people or to themselves, that they want to become a writer, as if it's a status or a profession where you get a degree and then you're a writer. Writers write. They can't help it. They can't not. At some point defeated, without readers, or without a subject, without something that calls out to be put into the world, without riding on the belief that nothing exactly the same has been in the world before, they might give up. Then they aren't writers. People sometimes ask writers if they're going to retire. You don't retire from writing any more than you retire from breathing. Perhaps at a certain point you can't do it anymore. For some people what stops them from writing is whatever it is that stops them from breathing. For ten months in 2022 that was how I lived; for ten months I didn't write a word that went into the world. I couldn't believe how easy it was.

Writing is rooted in memory: in some alchemy of responses, particular to everyone, with no one's translation of life the same. My writing is rooted in a doubled memory. It's a memory of an actual incident, but inside that memory is a false memory, an attempt to remember something that can't be found.

I was ten in 1955. My family had just moved into a new house in Menlo Park, now famous as the site of the headquarters of Facebook, then famous for nothing.

People might tell you it was named for the town in New Jersey where Thomas Edison invented the phonograph. In our house, in a library room where you could squirrel yourself off from everyone else, there was a big tube radio console, and I'd play with the radio at night, trying to pull in the drifting AM signals from stations across the country, from Salt Lake City, Cincinnati, even dance bands from hotels in New Jersey, as if that made some kind of loop back to where I was. One night, a few lines came out. "When American GIs left Korea," the radio said, "they also left behind countless fatherless babies. Once, everyone talked about this. Now, nobody cares."

Those words bothered me at the time, but I put them out of my mind. Or so I thought. For the next twenty years, that radio incident would reappear — crashing into whatever I was thinking like an invisible meteorite. As I got older, I realized this was an echo of something other than what the words on the radio actually described — I knew it was an echo of an absent memory, a phantom memory of my own father, whose name was Greil Gerstley, who was lost in a typhoon in the Pacific when his destroyer went down. Those were all of the facts present at the time, and for so long after: no date, no details, no story. I was born Greil Gerstley, but when those words came out of the radio, I wasn't Greil Gerstley anymore. And although those words made me an echo chamber for the memory they called up, I had nothing to remember: the memory that was called up was silent and blank.

Still, we all have memories of things we didn't experience: cultural memories that have taken up residence in our minds, built houses, filled them with furniture and appliances, and commanded that we live in them. I never saw Ty Cobb or Babe Ruth play, but they were as real to me growing up as President Eisenhower: I was raised with tales of their hero sagas, even the story of a great-aunt who supposedly slept with Babe Ruth, even with the fact that, when I was a baseball history–mad ten-year-old, Ty Cobb himself lived in Menlo Park. (Afraid he might spike me, I never knocked on his door; I did send him a postcard for an autograph, which he sent back with a signature so fresh-looking it could have been made in 1911, when, my baseball Hall of Fame book said, he hit .420. Many years later, I found that his door was open: friends of mine were at his house all the time, asking for the old-timer stories he was happy to tell. What I wouldn't give now to have had a little more nerve in 1955!)

These sorts of memories, these cultural memories, come to us from all sources, but especially from movies. There is that blank memory, but what explained it to me, as if it lay behind it, was one particular movie: David Lynch's *Blue Velvet*.

The famous opening of this 1986 picture seems to parody the American fantasy of home, peace, quiet, and appliances — that is, the all-but-trademarked American dream. But what's most interesting about what's happening on the screen is that it may have no satiric meaning at all.

The title sequence has shown a blue velvet curtain, swaying slightly from some silent breeze, casting back to the black-and-white velvet or satin backgrounds of the opening credits for 1940s B pictures. The theme music is ominous, alluring, at first suggesting Hitchcock's *Vertigo,* then a quiet setting where predictability has replaced suspense, then horns cutting off all hints of a happy ending. Bobby Vinton sings "Blue Velvet," his soupy number-one hit from 1963 — but with the sound hovering over slats of a white picket fence with red roses at their feet, the song no longer sounds soupy, or for that matter twenty-three years in the past. It sounds clean and timeless, just as the white of the fence and the red of the roses, shot from below, so that you look up at them as if at a flag, are so vivid you can barely see the objects for the colors. For an instant, the viewer is both visually and morally blinded by the intensity of the familiar; defenses are stripped away.

In slow motion, a fireman on a fire engine moving down a well-kept middle-class street waves at you, a warm smile on his moon face. Another picket fence, now with blazing yellow tulips. Children cross a street in an orderly manner as a middle-aged crossing guard holds up her stop sign. There is a house with a white picket fence and a middle-aged man watering the lawn. Inside the house a middle-aged woman sits on a sofa; there's a Pierrot doll on the lamp behind her. She's drinking coffee and watching an old-fashioned television, a small screen in a blond wooden box with legs, a set from the 1950s, when a TV was sold as a piece of furniture, in this case an object reflecting values of taste and modesty, and also modest enough that the man in the yard might have made the box himself. A crime picture is on. The hand of a man carrying a gun crosses the screen.

Outside, the man watering the lawn seems to sway with Bobby Vinton. The camera shows the faucet where the garden hose is attached leaking spray. The hose catches on a branch. The sound of water coming from the hose and the faucet rises to a rumble that seems to be coming out of the ground. Every predictable gesture is about to shatter from the pressure the predictable is meant to hide. The man clutches his neck and falls to the ground. A dog rushes up, plants its forefeet on the groin of the prone man, and drinks from the spray. The rumble grows stronger. The camera goes down to the ground, beneath the grass, to reveal a charnel house, the secret world, where armies of hideous beetles, symbols of human depravity, of men and women as creatures of absolute appetite, an appetite that banishes all conscience, appear to rise up and march out of the ground to take over the world like the ants in *Them!* Then the hero finds an ear in a field and the detective story that will take up the rest of the movie begins.

But it's the pastoral that stays in the mind, not the nightmare bugs and things-are-not-as-they-seem. Rather, Lynch's portrayal of things-as-they-ought-to-be feels too elegant to gainsay. It feels whole, not like a cheat. As an obvious contrivance it carries its own reality, because as a mock-up it fixes the real street. For its moment, it feels like a step out of the theater and into an idea of real life. Watching the movie for a second or third time, you can see that the slightly stiff framing and timing of the fireman, the children, the crossing guard, the too-bright images of fences and flowers, are a matter not of making the familiar strange but of getting at how familiar the familiar actually is.

The shots don't play like a dream, and they don't play like the beginning of an exciting new story. They play like memory, and they stay in the mind like a common memory laying itself over whatever personal memories a person watching might bring to the images — because what the sequence seems to be showing is a proof that the notion of personal memory is false. The details of the sequence could perhaps be excavated to match specific details of David Lynch's own boyhood, but what is striking about these quiet, burningly intense images is that nothing in them is specific to anyone. They are specific — overwhelmingly specific — only as images of the United States.

Anyone's memory is composed of both personal and common memories, and they are not separable. Memories of incidents that seem to have actually happened, once, in a particular time, to you, are colored, shaped, even determined, which is to say fixed in your memory, by the affinities your personal memories have to common memories: common memories as they are presented in textbooks and television programs, comic strips and movies, slang and clothes, all the rituals of everyday life as they are performed in one country as opposed to the way they are performed somewhere else.

The images that open *Blue Velvet* are images of things anyone watching a movie made in the USA can be presumed to have seen before, in actual experience or in TV shows or for that matter other movies, to have remembered as if they waved back at the fireman or picked up the hose – as if whatever it is that makes the image significant was determined by the person remembering it, and no one else. But this is not true – and you can take it farther. If personal memory is false, what happens when you try to construct a memory of something that, in fact, you do not remember, but should – that you desperately want to remember?

I think I always knew that the words about the Korean orphans, left behind and forgotten in the United States, lay behind what I ended up doing with my life: rewriting the past, pursuing an obsession with secret histories, with stories untold – with what, to me, were deep, fraternal connections between people who never met or even heard of each other. Such people — as in my second book, from 1989 — as the dadaist Richard Huelsenbeck in Zurich in 1916, the essayist Guy Debord in Paris in 1954, and the punk singer Johnny Rotten in London in 1976. Once, a person interviewing me about that book, the poet Lorenzo Buj, asked me about some lines I'd written there: "Lost children seek their fathers, and fathers seek their lost children, but nobody really looks like anybody else. So all, fixed on the wrong faces, pass each other by." He asked me if I was one of those sons or fathers. I told him that what he was quoting was one of those things any writer stumbles on, that I found those lines and kept them because they made sense of what I was trying to set out at that point in the book, with no personal motive — and that it was only later, rereading that passage, that I realized it was made up of the most autobiographical or confessional words in the book. I thought I was solving a problem on the page. I have a strong sense of privacy; in this case I didn't want to reveal myself to myself, but instead I revealed myself to anyone who chose to read what I had written. "We think we know what we're doing," the Brains sang in "Money Changes Everything" in 1978. They finished the line: "We don't pull the strings."

One can of course remember what one hasn't experienced. Older people tell children, *This is what he was like, this is the song he loved, this is how he laughed, how he walked, the team he rooted for.* You absorb that; you meet the person who in fact you will never meet, and so that person, never present, becomes part of your memory. But in my case, none of that was true.

I was born six months and a day after my father was killed in the Second World War: legally, born an orphan. I know that now, but growing up, I never had a date to hold on to, to build from. My mother, born Eleanore Hyman, was from San Francisco; Greil Gerstley, in 1944, at twenty-four, executive officer on the destroyer the *Hull,* second in command, was from Philadelphia. They hadn't known each other long when they married in San Francisco on September 7. My mother went with my father to Seattle, where the *Hull* shipped out.

I was left with the name, which became, for me, a talisman and a mystery. In 1948 my mother remarried, to Gerald Marcus, a San Francisco lawyer who grew up in San Jose, and he adopted me, and my name was changed. I don't remember myself as Greil Gerstley, but Greil was an inescapable name — I always had to explain it, but I really had nothing to tell. The story of the *Hull* was not told in my family. There were no pictures of my father Greil Gerstley in my house. When I visited my Philadelphia family, there were pictures, but I felt furtive, unfaithful, criminal, when I looked at them, and no one ever offered me a picture of my own to keep. There were memories—I was visiting my grandfather and my father's older brother and sister. There were letters my father wrote to other family members: in one he described how Bing Crosby's recording of "Blues in the Night" was the only thing that got him through the day. There was even a professionally shot home movie, showing my father in his dress Navy uniform—in the way he looked, in the casual, commanding way he wore his dress Navy cap, so much a match, now, for John F. Kennedy that the footage is hard to look at—but none of that was shared with me. It must have been that to tell the story of who my father was, what he had done, what happened to him and to so many others, would have been too much for a small boy to take on—or that to tell me such things would be, somehow, a breach of faith with my new father, or with my mother, in her new life.

The situation never changed. When I grew older, the habit of not speaking about the past became a kind of prison. I didn't know how to break out of it. I didn't ask, and nobody told. My own daughters might ask my mother what it was like to have been married to someone else; I never could. Like many children, I sometimes fantasized that I was not the child of my parents — but in my case, it was at least half true. Or more than half true.

Though I always knew I had a different father than my brothers and my sister, if my father had lived my mother would never have lived the life I came from; none of my siblings would have been born. When, at first, I asked about my father, she would say she didn't remember. Their time together had been so short, she said. The letters he wrote her from the *Hull* — he was in charge of censoring mail, which meant he could say what he pleased — were thrown out. He might have told her that, one night, preparing a navigation chart, he named a star after her, but if he did she never told me. My mother gave her wedding book to her mother — and when, sometime in the mid-1950s, my grandmother took it out and paged through it with me, she told me never to tell my mother she had showed it to me.

So in times of childhood or teenage unhappiness, the fantasy that I might have lived a different life, been a different person with a different name, was more a fact than a fantasy. But it was the kind of fact that, when you try to hold on to it, slips through your fingers like water.

So I developed my obsession with the past. I read the history books in the Landmark Books series, from *The First Men in the World* by Anne Terry White in 1953 to *The Witchcraft of Salem Village* by Shirley Jackson in 1956 and on from there. They were hardback books; they probably cost about $1.50. I'd read one in a day and then I'd read it again. I used the cultivated mystery of my own past as a spur to reconstructing events as they happened, and as they didn't — as they might have. This is always the route I've traveled, whether writing about Elvis Presley or Bill Clinton, Bob Dylan or Huey Long, about the life Robert Johnson might have lived if he hadn't been murdered in Mississippi in 1938, the life the Houston blues singer Geeshie Wiley could have lived if she hadn't disappeared not long after she made records in 1930, about John Wayne in *Rio Bravo* or Frank Sinatra in *The Manchurian Candidate*. Events as they happened, and as they didn't; when in 1964, at nineteen, during the Free Speech Movement at Berkeley, when it seemed everyone was reading Camus's *The Rebel*, somebody handed me a copy, the 1956 Vintage paperback edition, and I was instantly transfixed.

I was staring at the cover. I tried to stare into it. My own unintelligible sense of history, never put into words, never fixed in an image, was staring back at me. A black-and-white drawing by the children's book illustrator Leo Lionni—black and gray, really—showed a crumpled newspaper blowing in the wind. There were unreadable headlines and stories in different languages and alphabets smeared on the single front page.

"If, finally, the conquerors succeed in molding the world according to their laws, it will not prove that quantity is king, but that this world is hell," Camus wrote in that book: "In this hell, the place of art will coincide with that of vanquished rebellions, a blind and empty hope in the pit of despair. Ernst Dwinger in his *Siberian Diary* mentions a German lieutenant—for years a prisoner in a camp where cold and hunger were almost unbearable—who constructed himself a silent piano with wooden keys. In the most abject misery, perpetually surrounded by a ragged mob, he composed a strange music which was audible to him alone. And for those of us who have been thrown into hell, mysterious melodies and the torturing images of a vanished beauty will always bring us, in the midst of crime and folly, the echo of that harmonious insurrection which bears witness, throughout the centuries, to the greatness of humanity." Except for that story, the picture on the cover stayed with me with more force and poetry than any sentences or ideas from the book itself. That drawing was history to me, it was language, it was real life as it happens. A paper flying down the street with headlines of rebellions and refusals and battles and defeats, blowing out of reach. You can see someone chasing the sheet down the street, as if it were the last bit of written evidence of the story of its times, full of sound and fury, gone with the wind, all the assassinations, massacres, failed social experiments, poetic negations, all the raised and dashed hopes of the century that left only these illegible traces in the world, which is, somehow, not nothing. "Shahid watched his lover across the bookshop, a spacious place on two floors with the stock displayed on huge tables; in the past bookstores had always been so dingy," Hanif Kureishi wrote in his novel *The Black Album*. "Seeing the piles of new volumes Shahid wanted to snatch them up, not knowing how he'd survived without them. Deedee bought *Lipstick Traces,* and he followed her to the till, awaiting the bookmark and bag."

I never expected my untold story to actually appear, as real life – to challenge, as real life, the fantasy that has always been the foundation for whatever it is I write.

But the story did appear. About thirty years ago, my father called to say there was a documentary on the *Hull* on the Weather Channel. My wife was out; I watched it alone. When she came back, I said, "I just saw my father die." He wasn't in the film; survivors from the *Hull* spoke over stock footage and still photos of the typhoon that killed more than four hundred men from their ship and four hundred from the two other ships that went down in the same storm. You saw their Navy photos, as they were in 1944; you saw them now, laughing, stoic, crying, speaking of the men who made it into the open sea with life jackets, and who, when they were found, had nothing of themselves left below the waist – countless men eaten by sharks. It was the greatest disaster in the history of the U.S. Navy.

A few years after that, a writer named Bruce Henderson got in touch with me. He was looking for information about Greil Gerstley for a book on the *Hull*. Was I perhaps named for him by a friend? Was I a distant relative? Was there anything I could tell him?

The story he told, based on interviews he had conducted with survivors and people in the orbit of the ship, was terrible. The *Hull* had been at Pearl Harbor on December 7, 1941, but not damaged. Its captain then — the man who trained my father — was respected and trusted. In Seattle, he was replaced by a martinet from Annapolis, a man so vain and incompetent, so impatient with advice from experienced officers and so sure of his own right way, that when the *Hull* set out for the South Pacific, twenty men went AWOL, certain that to ship with this man was a death sentence.

With the typhoon looming, Admiral William Halsey — "Bull" Halsey — ordered the fleet to sail into it: "To see what they're made of." My grandfather Isaac Gerstley once saw Halsey in a restaurant. He went up to him. "You killed my son," he said.

With the ship trapped in a trough, with waves on each side a hundred feet high, the captain determined to power the engines to full throttle and smash his way out, while his officers tried to tell him that, in a trough, you cut the engines and wait. The captain panicked. He issued contradictory orders, rescinded them, issued them again. Other officers, who survived to tell the story to Bruce Henderson, begged my father — who was trusted as the captain was not, admired as the captain was reviled — to seize the ship: to place the captain under arrest, take command, and save the ship, in other words to lead a mutiny. There was no mutiny, but Herman Wouk was also in the typhoon, and heard the stories: *The Caine Mutiny* was based on what happened on the *Hull,* and what might have happened.

My father refused. In the history of the Navy there had never been a mutiny, he said. He knew, he said, that if he didn't take command he and everyone else would probably die, and if he did, and they lived, "That son of a bitch will have us all hung."

The ship was pitching at angles of seventy degrees. My father was thrown against machinery, breaking ribs, bones in his back, and the bones of one hand. A sailor got a splint on his hand. The ship pitched over ninety degrees — and after that the only direction it could go was down. With the ship flooding, my father was pulled from a hatch into the open sea. One survivor says he said to a sailor who approached him, "Don't try to help me, I won't make it." Another remembers him asking for help, and the men near him knowing he had no chance.

As it happens, long after the war, when enough time had passed for those who had been part of it to talk about it, the survivors of the *Hull* began to hold reunions. In December 2006, in Las Vegas, they held

GREIL ISAAC GERSTLEY, 1920–1944

what they determined would be their last, and my older daughter went. She looked like Greil Gerstley, as I don't; my mother, in a rare unguarded moment, was the first to see it. The people in Las Vegas saw it.

They told her stories, some of them as awful as the one Bruce Henderson told: that when the original captain of the *Hull* was told, by one of the survivors, that if he had still been the captain, the ship would never have gone down, he shot himself.

So now I know these facts, or I have heard, second- and third-hand, these stories. I have a story I can tell. I'm telling it now. If it had been told to me when I was a child, I might have, in a true sense, remembered it as if I had been there, with the same instantly recallable immediacy with which I can recite the exploits of Ty Cobb and Babe Ruth. But these facts, severed from the family history that could have given them flesh, and still made spectral by the family life I actually lived, are, really, no more mine than the images that open *Blue Velvet*.

I can make sense of them, or hold them in my mind, only as scenes from movies—the likes of *The Cruel Sea, Victory at Sea*, the documentaries *The World at War* or *Why We Fight*—or from the *Hull* movie that, someday, someone might make. But if any such movie were made, the story that I have, as a personal story, would be even less mine than it is now — and the truth is that it isn't mine at all. It is a contrivance — it is a story that I might remember, but don't. What might have been a personal story dissolves into the public domain of a greater story, of the War, of heroism and stupidity, arrogance and decency and hundreds of thousands of the dead — and in that sense, whatever personal memory might be found there, the common memory rightly takes away.

What is left one might call neurosis, or fixation, or even a haunting — and it can be used. I've used it all my life, more or less consciously, less consciously as I've gotten older, as a form of energy, as an impetus, as a way of looking at the world: why I write. For a long time, I thought it was that simple: a nice, organized mise en scène I could use as I chose. But one night in 2023, thinking about all this, trying to fall asleep, instead of trying to remember state capitals or the A to Z streets in Minneapolis, I began to go over words from the titles and part titles of my books, and it all stared back at me like the open mouth of a nightmare killer in a horror movie:

MYSTERY

AMERICA

STRANDED

DESERT ISLAND

SECRET

HISTORY

DEAD

OBSESSION

DUSTBIN

FASCIST

INVISIBLE

REPUBLIC

DEATH

LOVE

LIBERTY

DISAPPEARANCE

FORGETTING

UNDER THE RED WHITE AND BLUE

PATRIOTISM

MYTH

Those words, many of them, arrived unbidden, just like the phrases that come down out of nowhere, appearing in front of me, daring me to say I wrote them when I know I didn't. The words *invisible* and *republic* made up a book title: the publishers in the U.S. and the U.K. didn't like my original title, so I wrote out a list of twenty in ten minutes and told them to choose whatever they liked. They both chose *Invisible Republic*. There was no thought involved at all — only that ghost Bob Dylan talked about, a trickster ghost. What I write for. Fun. Play. Discover.

Play that Brains song again.

2

Pauline Kael

I write because in 1966 I read Pauline Kael. A very used paperback of her first book, *I Lost It at the Movies* — I caught the innuendo, but was too naïve to believe it — was lying around the Berkeley hills house on Panoramic Way I was sharing with three other students. I was shocked by it: by the total engagement of a writer with her subject, which might first take the form of a movie and then expand to take in, or maybe create, the whole social world that movie would have to address, surrender to, or defy. It felt like the most exciting writing I'd ever read. Whatever picture she was writing about, even if she was exposing all of its weaknesses and compromises, she made it clear how high the stakes could be, for an artistic and social failure as much as for a work that might leave whoever was watching changed, and unsatisfied with anything poorer. I wanted to know what it would be to feel as alive as the person in these pages had to have been to have written them. It's a question I'm still trying to answer.

I write criticism. When I started, in 1968, with that first *Rolling Stone* record review, I don't think I even knew the word, at least as it referred to some kind of writing, or some kind of thinking. Anyway, it seemed pompous and pretentious, as if it were a form of expertise. I didn't want that. I was a fan, writing out of fandom, out of love and betrayal: You have to hear this! This is a fraud! You have to hear this even more! Then one day in late 1969, given my suzerainty as the Records editor, I assigned myself the forthcoming Rolling Stones album, *Let It Bleed*. I heard it, I read it, as much more than another Rolling Stones album, though in those days, in that world, every Rolling Stones album was an event, a summing up, a document of where the world its listeners lived in and were trying to make was at that moment. But this was more. It had a longer look back, and a longer gaze forward. It was about — or it was an attempt to enact — the close of a chapter in history, of the idea, already being sold as a brand, of "The Sixties," a period in which people living it historicized it as they did so.

It did more than that. What that was Stanley Booth caught in 2000, writing about the Rolling Stones' American tour he covered as I was first listening to *Let It Bleed:* "In the sixties we believed in a myth — that music had the power to change people's lives. Today we believe in a myth — that music is just entertainment." From its first song, "Gimme Shelter," to its last, "You Can't Always Get What You Want," the music on *Let It Bleed* said that a thrilling time when anything seemed possible was about to turn to stone, and open into a future of dread and terror, into a realm where to speak falsely, or even carelessly, could be fatal, body and soul. And I found to get that down, to get at what was going on with Mick Jagger's voice and Keith Richards's guitar, I had to broaden the context of the music as far as I could. I had to write about photography and movies and fiction and every form of cultural speech that was feeding into the album and bleeding out of it.

That was when I got an idea of what criticism is and what it could be. It was an analysis of one's own response to something out there in the world, in this case a $3.98 LP. Why am I reacting to this so intensely? Why does it make me smile and scare me at the same time? Does it matter if he's saying "death" or "bed," or is it the way the word slides away as it's sung where the real meaning of the moment lies, where it takes place, and does David Bailey's portrait of Marianne Faithfull ask the same question and leave the answer even more open?

To ask these questions was a claim of cultural citizenship: not only do I have the right to say in public what I think this is and why that matters, I have an obligation to do it. Listen to me; I'll listen to you.

That was the beginning of what I have done with my life since: when I saw what criticism could be and what it might take to realize it. It was again, a dare: as a writer, you can make the world bigger and more interesting, and as a writer live in that world, and find a life's work, or you can shrink everything down to your own crabbed and paltry self, hang on for years conning editors and publishers and yourself, and find a life's lie.

That was one beginning. But I remember even more clearly the first critical event I ever witnessed — a foundation stone worth as much to me as that record review that opened onto all the pages I've written since.

Nineteen sixty-two was the year I found out there was more to movies than rooting for the good guys and cowering in your seat. I saw Bergman's *The Seventh Seal* and I saw the devil dancing the dead over the crest of a hill. I saw Dryer's *The Passion of Joan of Arc*—I saw Falconetti in a performance that almost erases Garbo.

I saw *The Manchurian Candidate,* probably the first American movie that could carry Fassbinder's title *Fear Eats the Soul.* But 1962 was also the year of a filmic incident I've recalled at least as often as I've thought of any of those classics, movies that have inspired whole books, novels, other films, all down their century and into the next: the night I saw *The Pirates of Blood River.*

It was the last day of school. The Park Theatre in Menlo Park was jammed with students, most of them graduating and a lot of them drunk. The air was thick with the tension oozing out of a thousand bodies; up on screen, evil pirates, noble Huguenots, and a lot of piranha gave chase to a progressively incomprehensible storyline. The movie was not delivering: four years of high school for a reward like this? Suddenly, with bullets shooting off in all directions and nobody caring, a tall kid stood up in one of the front rows, turned to face the crowd, and raised his arms. "I NOMINATE

THE PIRATES OF BLOOD RIVER (1961), DIRECTED BY JOHN GILLING,
COLUMBIA PICTURES (ALBUM / ALAMY STOCK PHOTO)

THIS MOVIE SHIT-FUCK OF THE YEAR, 1962!"
he roared—and just like that the release everyone had
come seeking was granted.

Four years later, I found that Pauline Kael book—
by the woman whose program notes for her Telegraph
Avenue double art house–theater shack the Cinema
Guild were taped on our refrigerator, just as they were
on half the refrigerators in town, though they weren't
signed, and I made no connection between the two. "A
savagely written book by America's most controversial
movie critic!" it said on the cover. I started reading.
It was a collection of criticism—reviews, portraits of
Hollywood and of the shadow country where the president was Marlon Brando, polemics, swooning celebra-
tions and implacable hit jobs. The writing jumped on
the page. There was an expansive, enlivening sense of
history underpinning a vast frame of cultural reference,
drawing at any moment on politics, music, dance, theater, literature. Never mind the movie: her piece on the
Terence Stamp–Robert Ryan film of *Billy Budd* dove
deeper into Melville's story than anything I'd read or
heard in college.

She all but shook on the page over *Fires on the
Plain.* She smiled on the page through *Jules and Jim.*
She cited *The Seventh Seal, The Passion of Joan of Arc,*

and *The Manchurian Candidate*. She did not mention *The Pirates of Blood River*. But because for Kael everything began with the experience of seeing a movie, the book had room for it, room for the kid standing up in front of the screen — or for the antiepiphanic explosion they could produce — as it had, and still has, room for anything else that might go into the experience of seeing a movie, arguing about it later, or remembering it years and years after that. "Criticism is exciting just because there is no formula to apply," she wrote in 1963 in "Circles and Squares," a precise, withering demolition in the Berkeley journal *Film Quarterly* of Andrew Sarris's trumpeting of critical formula in his "Notes on the Auteur Theory in 1962" in the New York journal *Film Culture* — "just because you must use everything you are and everything you know."

> When *Shoeshine* opened in 1947, I went to
> see it alone after one of those terrible lovers'
> quarrels that leave one in a state of incom-
> prehensible despair. I came out of the the-
> ater, tears streaming, and overheard the
> petulant voice of a college girl complaining
> to her boyfriend, "Well I don't see what was

so special about that movie." I walked up the street, crying blindly, no longer certain whether my tears were for the tragedy on the screen, the hopelessness I felt for myself, or the alienation I felt from those who could not experience the radiance of *Shoeshine*. For if people cannot feel *Shoeshine,* what *can* they feel? . . . Later I learned that the man with whom I had quarreled had gone the same night and also emerged in tears. Yet our tears for each other, and for *Shoeshine* did not bring us together. Life, as *Shoeshine* demonstrates, is too complex for facile endings.

Kael wrote as a member of the audience, as alive to the people around her as she was to what was on the screen — that, I found, was how I wanted to write, who I wanted to be. "I don't care if he is a genius," she heard someone say in 1953. "I don't like that man." That went into the first words she got into print, "Some Notes on Chaplin's *Limelight.*" For years, until someone took the trouble to dig it out of the archives, the story went that that first review was titled "Slimelight": that was what the poet Robert Duncan called the picture when he and Kael walked out of the theater. The word doesn't appear in her piece. Published that year in *City Lights,* a journal that, like the San Francisco bookstore that put it out, was named for another Chaplin movie, Kael's review is still harsh enough to bring the reader up short decades upon decades later, when *The Gold Rush* and *The Great Dictator* and *Modern Times* are still screened around the world and *Limelight* is forgotten.

At the end of the 1931 silent film *City Lights,* Chaplin's tramp leaves prison so filthy and destroyed you don't want to look at him. He walks the streets, picking butts out of the gutter, and then, as James Agee wrote in 1949, "the blind girl who has regained her sight, thanks to the Tramp, sees him for the first time. . . . She recognizes who he must be by his shy, confident, shining joy as he comes silently toward her. And he recognizes himself, for the first time, through the terrible changes in her face. The camera just exchanges a few quiet close-ups of the emotions which shift and intensify in each face. It is enough to shrivel the heart to see, and it is the greatest piece of acting and the highest moment in movies."

That Chaplin was nowhere in sight in 1953; Kael tracked him to his hiding place in his own movie, in his own ego. Re-creating the context in which the movie was made and in which a certain movie lover paid her money and sat down to wait for the picture to begin — with the sense of time and place, here, not there, now, not then, that over the next years would draw so many readers into real or imaginary conversations with her — she began in the audience, listening to the talk of the people around her, imagining herself talking to them. Her critical premise was not that she possessed special knowledge, though she did. It began with a sense of herself as any movie's ideal watcher: no better or worse than anyone else, as she sat in her seat, but maybe better out of it, because while everyone else got up and went about their lives, Kael stayed in the audience, even when she went home. It's always been the way I understand whatever it is I do: the premise wasn't that her ideas about a movie would be deeper than those of other people, but that other people were *busy* — so she would draw on their reactions as well as her own and, as she wrote, put people back in the theater, as if she were providing a running commentary as they all watched together. That has been my goal, my writer's utopia.

Kael looked at Calvero, the aging comedic saint Chaplin was playing in *Limelight,* and as the conceit of the character turned into its own bad joke, she came to life as a critic. The cruel wit, the natural reach from one medium to another, the sense of betrayal – the free-swinging, freewheeling yawp of the artistic citizen – it was all there from the start: "Calvero's gala benefit in which he shows the unbelievers who think him finished that he is still the greatest performer of them all, his death in the wings as the applause fades – this is surely the richest hunk of gratification since Huck and Tom attended their own funeral."

What nails it? What is it that signals the arrival of a new voice, impatient, in love with her subject and as keen to its betrayals as its promises, speaking American? "Hunk."

Writing from Berkeley, picking up steam from then on, her artistic ambition rising, the whole terrain of the movies as they had been, what they were, what they could be, opening up before her, as she shared her pages with the people who surrounded her in the theaters, she did the same with the academics and poets and painters she argued with. She shared her pages with the New York critics who handed down the word that, as a single mother trying to make herself heard in any forum that would give her space and freedom, and sometimes even money, she so gleefully tossed back.

"A lady critic," from "far-off San Francisco," Sarris wrote in 1968 in his *The American Cinema,* unable, after that "Circles and Squares" (he had presented the auteur theory as a series of circles of meaning, but in Kael's piece he was the square), to bring himself to mention her by name. *Can you imagine! A woman! From San Francisco!*

Paying her money like anybody else, Kael walked out of the theater transformed or humiliated—the humiliation you feel when you get to the end and realize you've been bamboozled into seeing something that makes you feel physically smaller, morally weaker, and stupid. "Robbe-Grillet," she wrote in 1964 of the screenwriter for the worshiped 1961 New Wave picture *Last Year at Marienbad,* "may say that the film is a pure construction, an object without reference to anything outside itself, and that the existence of the two characters begins when the film begins and ends ninety-three minutes later, but, of course, we are not born when we go in to see a movie—though we may want to die by the time we leave." Kael made prissy critics like Sarris uncomfortable because she demanded more out of movies, out of life, than they did. She demanded everything—that was how I learned that there were no limits to what a movie or a novel or a song could say, and no limits on what you could say about it.

It was easy to find yourself in Kael's essays; it was harder to get out of them. As with *West Side Story:*

> Sex is the great leveler, taste the great divider. I have premonitions of the beginning of the end when a man who seems charming or at least remotely possible starts talking about movies. When he says, "I saw a great picture a couple of years ago — I wonder what you thought of it?" I start looking for the nearest exit. His great picture generally turns out to be *He Who Must Die* or something else that I detested — frequently a socially conscious problem picture of the Stanley Kramer variety. Boobs on the make always try to impress with their high level of seriousness (wise guys, with their contempt for *all* seriousness).
>
> It's experiences like that that drive women into the arms of truckdrivers — and, as this is America, the truckdrivers all too often come up with the same kind of

status-seeking tastes: they want to know
what you thought of *Black Orpheus* or *Never
on Sunday* or something else you'd much
rather forget.

Summoning the mood of the country, the whole
arc of common life from the Depression through the
postwar boom, carrying the past and in pursuit of the
new, Kael could pull characters right out of the screen.
In 1955, in "The Glamour of Delinquency," on the punks
in *Blackboard Jungle,* James Dean in *East of Eden,* Marlon
Brando in *On the Waterfront:* "The delinquent is disturbing because he is delinquent from values none of us
really believe in; he acts out his indifference to what we
are all somewhat indifferent to. . . . Though films take
up social discontent only to dissolve it in unconvincing
optimism, the discontent has grown out of that optimism." You could dismiss this as sociology, not movie
criticism, if it didn't change the way you see the movies
Kael is writing about — or if you could find a sociolo-
gist who spoke so plainly. And the same verve, the same
claim that the terrain of criticism was the whole terrain of the society to which it was addressed, was there
in her long review of *Bonnie and Clyde,* which when it

appeared in the *New Yorker* in 1967 made me and so many others sit up with a shock of recognition: This is what criticism can be! This is how you do it!

Directed by Arthur Penn, written by David Newman and Robert Benton, starring Warren Beatty and Faye Dunaway as Clyde Barrow and Bonnie Parker—the real-life Depression-era outlaws whose gang of bank robbers and thieves centered on Texas, Oklahoma, Missouri, and Arkansas, but from 1932 to 1934 ranged from Minnesota to Colorado, leaving nine law officers and three more people dead before Barrow, at twenty-five, and Parker, at twenty-three, were torn to pieces in a police ambush in Louisiana—on release the picture was attacked on all sides as irredeemably violent, as a glamorization of crime and murder that might lead others to follow its heroes and threaten the social order and the morals of the nation. Even thoughtful critics wondered whether work like this should be put before the public, or even allowed under the law: "Too many people—including some movie reviewers— want the law to take over the job of movie criticism; perhaps what they really want," Kael said, "is for their own criticisms to have the force of law." That was where the picture stood, on the brink of a disapprobation so sweeping it implied that anyone who liked it was some-one you wouldn't want in your house — *who knows where else that mind has been?* Kael set out to fight for it.

Not many critics, in that first onrush, noticed what Kael did: that audiences were alive to the film as it played. She saw them left speechless, silenced, after its final massacre — because in the movie they could instinctively, almost physically feel that, set more than thirty years before, in some ways in the foreign country of the past, with Model Ts and corny banjo music and guns that seemed comically too big for the people using them, this was a movie set precisely in the present. That it was a picture of the USA in and of its time, that it was a refusal of or even an attack on the same author-ity fighting black Americans in their own streets, the same president: the same president who, as Bob Dylan rewrote him in 1965 in his "Tombstone Blues," towered over the nation, even taking on the sun. "The sun's not yellow, it's chicken!" Dylan's Lyndon Johnson's Icarus declared in Dylan's State of the Union address, because the sun wouldn't shine on LBJ's chicken-run in Vietnam. People saw the movie, and they saw, along with the snap in Faye Dunaway's voice and the fog of stupidity in Warren's Beatty's hotshot crook, that it captured, as

Dylan also said much later, the eye of a time in which "there were people trying to stop the show in any kind of way they could. . . . Then, you didn't know which end the trouble was coming from. And it could come at any time." They saw that it put on the screen what some people, in the moment, were doing or were about to do: robbing banks to pay for the revolution, for people to rise up and overthrow not only the government, but yes, the social order. It put on the screen what a lot more people than that lay awake at night thinking about, wishing they had the nerve to do it, and imagining that maybe they, too, could look as good as Warren Beatty and Faye Dunaway looked doing it. Kael said this was right, this was proper, this is what movies were supposed to do: to excavate the secret wishes and fears of their audience and put that audience on the spot. She uncovered the ways that all of the comedy in the film as it opened and seemed to set its terms was a setup, until people laughing in the theater "catch the first bullet right in the face." Why were people reacting, and what was the job of the critic in a critical moment like this? Not just to tell the truth, but to find the words and the arrangements of words to make the hidden clear, the forbidden plain, the argument not just convincing but, as thinking, thinking in public, which is what critics pay themselves to do, thrilling on its own terms, and her own terms. As she wrote at the outset of her seven thousand–word polemic–cum–essay–cum–critical argument–cum–critical entertainment, as she and the rest of the country left the theater and started talking about what they'd just seen,

> *Bonnie and Clyde* brings into the almost frighteningly public world of movies things that people have been feeling and saying and writing about. And once something is said or done on the screens of the world, once it has entered mass art, it can never again belong to a minority, never again be the private possession of an educated, or "knowing" group. But even for that group there is an excitement in hearing its own private thoughts expressed out loud and in seeing something of its own sensibility become part of our common culture.

So Kael wrote as a critical citizen, as a critical patriot, as opposed to the critics who cultivated their outrage and raised the question of what should be banned precisely because it might become part of a common culture. She wrote not as a censorious but as a poetic guardian of values. She wrote at the end as she had written to start:

> Once something enters mass culture, it travels fast. In the spoofs of the last few years, everything is gross, ridiculous, insane; to make sense would be to risk being square. A brutal new melodrama is called *Point Blank* and it is. So are most of the new movies. This is the context in which *Bonnie and Clyde,* an entertaining movie that has some feeling in it, upsets people — people who didn't get upset even by *Mondo Cane.* Maybe it's because *Bonnie and Clyde,* by making us care about the robber lovers, has put the sting back into death.

But note how the paragraph works; I spent, I realize now, years of critical practice figuring out how it works. The paragraph may end with a flourish, but it doesn't overpraise what she's talking about; she barely praises it at all. Throughout her piece, she focuses on where the film goes wrong, where it falls short, where it compromises, where it cheats: if Warren Beatty can fit an idea of a thirties gangster in his face and clothes, Faye Dunaway's haircut and makeup make her as 1967 as Marianne Faithfull. Kael brings out who is miscast, who overacts and who doesn't, and why the auteur-theory elevation of the director deforms our own sense of what brings a movie, or a single scene, or even a half-line of dialogue, to a version of life that can't be found anywhere else. What she wrote was a road map to essaying an argument that would build its credibility by adding detail to detail, refusing to compromise itself by glossing over flaws and wrong choices to make a point, to exchange criticism for propaganda. So she went carefully through the many previous movie versions of the Bonnie and Clyde story, through Arthur Penn's career as a director, looking for the strengths and flaws in the sensibility he brought to bear. She traced the loop of the aesthetic the screenwriters brought to Penn, the way thirties American crime pictures captivated the critics and then filmmakers of France's New Wave, how Godard's *Breathless* and Truffaut's *Shoot the Piano Player* gave Robert Benton and David Newman their own purchase on the story of thirties gangsters. She tracked Warren Beatty's career, going back to the dim, irresistible teenager of *Splendor in the Grass* to the grown-up art-house arty fool of *Mickey One,* finding his weaknesses and his strengths, what led him to the place where he could make the movie he as both star and producer had now made, and finding what she was after in places no one else, it seemed, was looking. For all the flair and intellectual weight of her opening and her close, this is my favorite passage in the piece, where Kael all but gets between the actor and the camera to open up a moment where a movie goes right or wrong, not trying to get you to open yourself to her argument about film and society, art and law, but just playing with movies, for the fun of seeing what they're made of, what makes cinematic moments stick in the mind and what lets them pass by with as little emotional effect as most of what happens in a day or a life:

> There is a story told against Beatty in a recent *Esquire* — how during the shooting of *Lilith* he "delayed a scene for three days demanding the line 'I've read *Crime and Punishment* and *The Brothers Karamazov*' be

changed to 'I've read *Crime and Punishment*
and *half* of *The Brothers Karamazov.*'"
Considerations of professional conduct
aside, what is odd is why his adversaries
waited three days to give in, because, of
course, he was right. That's what the character he played should say; the other way, the
line has no point at all.

When I finished that piece in the *New Yorker* — first
rejected by the *New Republic* as too long, though you
can read *too much* between the words, it would kick off
her twenty-three years as a *New Yorker* film critic — I felt
as if I had read someone who was both the map and
the territory: how to do it, but also why. If she showed
me what criticism was made of, and occupied her own
terrain, she showed me how I could understand what
I might bring to an ongoing critical conversation, and
how to open up my own territory, and let the cattle
kings and the farmers on my own Powder River, what I
could do and what I couldn't, fight it out.

What hit me when I first read that battered paperback in 1966 — the front showed a Hollywood couple
covered in makeup and money kissing fulsomely on a

giant screen, with, at the bottom of the image, in the seats below, the tiny silhouettes of a boy and a girl with their lips almost but not quite touching — did not exactly have to do with its perspicacity, anger, or the love that, in her pages, simply reading her on *Jules and Jim,* made it hard not to fall in love: with the movie, with Catherine and Jules and Jim, their love for one another, or with the person sitting next to you. It was that the book made a great promise, and paid its promise in full: "You must use everything you are and everything you know." On page after page, Kael moves to match that pledge, to test its limits. I read the book. I put it down. I picked it up again. Nearly sixty years later, I still read it, and with the same repeating sense of wonder: what would it feel like to write like that — to care that much?

I can't put it more directly. I didn't want to become a writer, even though, without understanding it, I already was. I became a writer because I wanted to feel as Pauline did when she wrote, and after all these formal pages I have to call her by her first name because we were friends. In 1976 I was writing a book column for *Rolling Stone,* and I'd written about her new book, *Reeling,* a collection of her *New Yorker* reviews from 1972 through 1975. The writing was out of control, I said, undercutting itself with gross superlatives, embarrassing neologisms that on the page sounded less like anything anyone ever said than words cooked up by an advertising agency: *It's zippy!* She called me up. She didn't wait on pleasantries. "Did you mean what you said about me in that review?" she said. What was I supposed to say? *No, I just wanted to look good by putting down a critic better known than I am?* "Yes," I said. "Well, my daughter agrees with you," she said. "But I don't." Humphrey Bogart has the next line.

3

Titian

I wrote earlier of a critical event, a critical confrontation with something outside of yourself where the world suddenly looks different, and you have to come to grips with it, you have to think about it, and a germ is planted and sooner or later you will have to write about it — in that case, seeing *Pirates of Blood River* in 1962. There are other critical events that have shaped my own sense of what writing can be and where it can go just as much. Maybe there are hundreds, thousands. But only a few really stand out.

Reading *Moby-Dick* for the third or fourth time and finding myself overwhelmed at the way a single line early in the book can bring the next two hundred pages rushing back as if I'd lived them myself—which, since this is a book, and you're supposed to read it, along with all the generations since 1851 I had. Listening to the Firesign Theatre's 1969 *How Can You Be in Two Places at Once When You're Not Anywhere at All* over and over from 1983 to 1988 while writing a book because every time I heard something I'd never heard before—never mind the critical event of then sitting in a radio station in Los Angeles in 1989 as two members of the four-man surrealist radio-play-recording-studio comedy group explained the book to me.

Reading *The Great Gatsby* for the twentieth time and still not quite believing that any ordinary person, drunk or sober, could have written ". . . a fresh, green breast of the new world. Its vanished trees, the trees that had made way for Gatsby's house, had once pandered in whispers to the last and greatest of all human dreams; for a transitory enchanted moment man must have held his breath in the presence of this continent, compelled into an aesthetic contemplation he neither understood nor desired, face to face for the last time in history with something commensurate to his capacity for wonder." It's a critical event that for me never ends: it was only a few years ago, reading that last page, that I saw the way the limitless floating image of the green breast of the new world then falls down, is taken down, to the paltry and impoverished image of the green light at the end of Daisy's dock, even if they are only a few lines apart, just as, writing this now, it was only in the moment that I noticed that that new world pandered in *whispers,* as if whispers had never been there before. There's something about the spell the book casts, the way it again and again conjures its own transitory enchanted moments, that makes a reader miss as they read, too carried away by one rhythm, the rhythm beneath it surfacing only at some other time.

There was the day in 1989 when I was merging on the freeway off the Bay Bridge toward Berkeley with "Gimme Shelter" on the radio, wondering what it was that had kept it coming out of the speakers for twenty years, wondering what made it seem absolutely new, in the strongest sense somehow unheard, and deciding, when I got home, that I would have to try to write about that, when a car cut in front of me and I had to change lanes without looking to avoid hitting it, and thinking, as my heart went back down to my chest when I realized the lane was clear, that if I had to go, there were worse ways.

There was a night in 1970 when, at the Palace of Fine Arts in San Francisco, on what I remember as a huge screen that was not a rectangle but a square, I saw F. W. Murnau's 1927 silent film *Sunrise: A Song of Two Humans*. Just as with Pauline Kael and *Bonnie and Clyde* I began to see what criticism could be, what it could do, there's a moment in *Sunrise* where the same thing happened — where I felt for the first time I was being given a glimpse of what movies themselves could be. The vamp stands up from the ground where she's seducing the farmer into murdering his wife for her. She begins to shimmy. *Sell your farm and come with me to the City!* — and then suddenly a shaking montage of noise and movement and jazz and dancing takes over the screen, everything happening at once, every image fading into and then rushing out of every other, smiles exploding over pounding drums, and a rush of air, the air of machines and electricity, blows through like a wind blowing trees and farms and rivers right off the map.

There was the day in 2013 when I walked into the Peggy Guggenheim museum in Venice and stopped in front of Jackson Pollock's 1947 *Alchemy,* one of his first poured paintings, one of his first experiments, or proofs, that by practicing an arcane art you really could turn not merely a few cans of household paint into millions of dollars, but turn something anyone might have in a garage into something no one could have predicted and that had anything been different on the day it was made would never have existed at all. I'd walked past it many times before, but this day I stopped. I stood up close and started looking at it, and then realized I couldn't. There was too much there, too much going on, too much movement, like the montage in *Sunrise,* which you can't see all at once either. I began to see, or think I did, that just as I can only remember *Sunrise* on a square screen, now I could begin to discern, to revelate, the intention hidden in the chance.

I decided I would divide the painting, eighty-seven inches long and forty-five inches high, into square inches, and look at them one at a time. I stood there trying to see into the first square inch in the top right corner. I did that for twenty minutes before realizing it would take the rest of my life, or another life on top of that, to traverse the whole thing.

In 2006, at the Cinema Ritrovato festival in Bologna, I was invited to present *The Manchurian Candidate* at the Piazza Maggiore — a huge square with a huge screen hung from a huge building under a blue-black sky. It had been my favorite movie since the first time I'd seen it, and I'd seen it dozens of times since. I wrote a book about it. I knew every line of dialogue, the way every scene was set and unfolded, and yet every time I saw it everything in it came with the uncanny sense that what was happening didn't have to happen, that there were a thousand choices between every word or gesture that didn't have to be made in the way that they were. There was always a sense that what was happening could be taken back—that at the end, with Frank Sinatra looking down from himself, as if he has to hide himself from himself, and cursing in shame and despair, "Hell. Hell," it didn't have to end the way it did.

The thousands of people watching were silent. As the movie headed toward its climax they were even more so, as if they had sucked the air out of the night, or the movie was sucking the air out of them. I knew what was coming, but I had never felt what then happened before. Was it the crowd, and the aura it gave off that the whole city, the whole word, history itself, was witnessing this event, and that this event was the end of the world? When Laurence Harvey's first bullet hits James Gregory's would-be president's forehead, and then when his second kills Angela Lansbury's mother, *his* mother, I felt as if the bullets were entering me. I couldn't move. I was pinned to my chair. After a seeming suspension in time, a long ovation rolled through the Piazza. People were cupping their hands around their mouths to join the sound, getting up to leave, but I couldn't move. I sat there, until everyone was gone, wanting with everything I had, more than I ever had before, for it all to come out differently. Finally I got up and walked through the empty backstreets of the city until I couldn't walk anymore.

All of those events and more have stayed with me. I've gone back to them, wondering what was going on, wondering at works of art, or the events they make as one looks and listens, again and again, trying to understand what they were saying and what, if I could, I could say to them. But none really measures up to the day I first saw Titian's *Assumption of the Virgin*.

I've always believed that the divisions between high art and low art—between high culture, which really ought to be called sanctified culture, and what's sometimes called popular culture, but ought to be called everyday culture—the culture of anyone's everyday life, the music that we listen to, the movies that we see, the museum objects we pass by or are fixed by, the advertisements that infuriate us and that sometimes we find so moving — are false. And as a result of trying to make that argument over the years, or by trying to work as if that argument is so true that it doesn't even have to be raised, I've come to believe that those divisions are permanent. They are as deeply embedded in our culture as racism and war. Those divisions can be denied, but they will never disappear.

The Museum of Modern Art in New York dramatized this quite fabulously in 1990 with a show called "High and Low." It presented famous pop art paintings, Philip Guston Krazy Kat and Roy Lichtenstein Steve Canyon and True Romance paintings, next to *Krazy Kat* comic strips and *Steve Canyon* or *True Romance* comic books.

The pop art paintings were definitely bigger than the comics panels — more dramatic. For that matter, they were more vulgar. But I couldn't understand then, and don't understand now, why George Herriman's *Krazy Kat* strips or the comic books produced by anonymous writers, inkers, and designers were lesser art — really, why they were not better art, the real art — than the pop art classics Philip Guston and Roy Lichtenstein made of them. I met Lichtenstein once, in his studio, walls and surfaces covered with comics and the mock-ups he had made out of them, ready to go. The whole scene reminded me of what Kirk Varnedoe, in 1990 the Chief Curator of Painting and Sculpture at MoMA, and co-curator of "High and Low," said in his companion book to the exhibition, *A Fine Disregard: What Makes Modern Art Modern*. The title – and the view of the world that it spoke for – came from a stone marker that stands at the gates of the Rugby School in England, one of the most aristocratic schools in the world. Varnedoe, who attended Rugby, placed all of modern art on this stone, which commemorates the exploits of one William Ellis Webb, who in 1823, "With," the stone says, "a fine dis-regard for the rules of football as played in his time, first took the ball in his arms and ran with it, thus inaugu-rating the distinctive feature of the rugby game." But the working word in the title is less "disregard" – for rules, expectations, and so on – than "fine." That is, one is being assured that modern art remains art. More than that, it remains the province of the sort of people who for centuries have attended the Rugby school – or who sit on the boards of art museums. One is being told modern art will not go too far – say "disregard" without the modifier and you have no idea what kind of riff-raff you might have to let in next.

Nearly everything I've written is based on the conviction, the learned belief, that there are depths and satisfactions, shocks and revelations, in blues, rock 'n' roll, detective stories, movies, and television, as rich and profound as those that can be found anywhere else.

In 2015, at the CUNY Graduate Center in New York, I took part in a public conversation with the late conservative philosopher and musicologist Roger Scruton. In his book *The Soul of the World,* about the disappearance of the sacred in modern life, and how it might be retrieved and restored, in a passage that I quoted back to him, he had defined music as "a perceived resolution of the conflict between freedom and necessity, made available in a space of its own" – "a reality that cannot be grasped from the ordinary cognitive standpoint." I said I thought that the dimension of the sacred, of what could not be grasped by the everyday unthinking mind, could be present in any music. I said that in pop music, blues, rock 'n' roll, jazz, where the listener, whether in solitary or face-to-face or a hundred rows back, can at any time be overcome with a sense of unlikeliness, of the listener's own inability to account for what is happening, of what they're hearing – that the listener is struck with a sense of awe, a sense of impossibility, a sense that something is taking place beyond intention, that the composer's or artist's or performer's intention cannot account for the sense one receives of the presence of some force outside the ordinary thinking mind, the intervention of some external intelligence or even gnosis. Scruton had spoken about standing at a train station that morning and how he was overwhelmed, to the point of feeling his humanity taken away, by the inundation of canned music, by EDM on boom boxes, by the mechanization of rhythm machines. I told him about an experience I'd had later that same day, at the 34th Street Herald Square subway station. Coming up the stairs, I heard someone playing an electric guitar. The sound was made with extraordinary confidence, it was atonal, notes were shattering in every direction, the volume was like a storm — it was tremendously abrasive and full of life. From the top of the stairs I walked down to an alcove to see who was making the noise: a middle-aged man wearing a crown with his name on it, Remy François. That conflict between freedom and necessity came into view: he was playing "House of the Rising Sun," and he was cutting it to pieces, breaking its back, but there was something about the melody of the song and the history it carried that held its shape, that could not be taken apart. Here was a song that goes back to the nineteenth century, that was first recorded in 1933 as "Rising Sun Blues" by the old-timey singers Clarence Ashley and Gwen Foster, was taken up by Bob Dylan in 1962 in a version he borrowed from the Greenwich Village folk singer Dave Van Ronk that two years later was heard by the Animals in Newcastle upon Tyne, who made it into a worldwide hit and brought it into the consciousness of people globally, and, I said, remained there as we were speaking. Remy François, I thought, was affirming the tradition the song had made by saying, in a way, that it could not be broken—and that there were infinite ways of seeing and feeling and taking meaning from that little concert.

Scruton demurred. "Let me be strictly honest," he said, speaking directly of music. "I think that the classical tradition, as I understand it, is the greatest achievement of Western civilization and it contains within it a reflection on the human condition that has no match elsewhere. That is a heretical view from a lot of standpoints, but that is what I think."

His demeanor and his certainty, the consideration that had gone into his statement of belief, demanded respect, but I didn't understand it—I didn't understand how one could live in that world. Who, I thought, leaving the conversation for questions from the audience, could argue that the sense of transportation, even in the religious sense — being taken out of one's self, connecting the self to something greater, something, you know in your heart, that every person ever born must experience or be left incomplete — is not as present in the third verse of "Gimme Shelter," as Merry Clayton pushes out of herself with a last *It's just a shot away,* with a pause between *It's* and *just* that speaks for a hesitation in the face of history, an immediate apprehension of its weight, that pause something between taking a breath and the appearance of a new idea — or the scene in *The Godfather* when the camera is moving in on Michael Corleone, so slowly, so inexorably, and Al Pacino says, "Then I'll kill them both" — as in any art, the most exalted in motive, the most revered in time?

Well, I believed all that when one day in 1996, on a first visit to Venice, following the advice of art-historian friends on what to see, I walked into the Basilica di Santa Maria Gloriosa dei Frari and saw Titian's *Assumption of the Virgin* — a sixteenth-century altarpiece painting of the Virgin Mary being borne up to heaven by scores of angels while people on the earth look up to her, God looks down, and the woman in the middle is caught somewhere between deliverance and terror. It was finished in 1518, twenty-six years after Columbus reached the New World, the most cataclysmic event in history. The painting was making a different argument. The most important event in history was the resurrection of Jesus Christ, and in this place was its mirror.

The painting is more than twenty-two feet high and more than eleven feet wide. As Pollock's *Alchemy* is too dense with the stuff of movement and history to see in a lifetime, this is so big you can barely take it in, no matter how close or far back you stand: big in size, but big in every other way, too — as will and idea, as drama and spectacle, space and time. I was stunned. I thought I knew something about art. I'd seen paintings all over the United States and Europe. I'd been moved to tears by some and scared by others. I'd seen hundreds of movies, listened to thousands of albums, some of them hundreds of times. I thought I knew something about art, and instantly I realized I knew nothing.

I was in shock. Again and again, I walked back and forth in front of the painting. I stopped and looked up at it. I walked to the back of the church to see it from a distance. I walked up to the base again. I did this many times.

TITIAN, *ASSUMPTION OF THE VIRGIN* (1516–18),
CHURCH OF SANTA MARIA GLORIOSA DEI FRARI, VENICE
(WIKIMEDIA COMMONS)

I kept trying to leave the building, and every time I reached the door I found myself pulled back in. I couldn't get out. I was trapped by revelation.

Yes, I said to myself, *I finally understand. The only great art is high art. And the only high art is religious art. And the only truly religious art is Christian art.* Three things that to the bottom of my life I don't believe — and I was reduced to a puddle of acceptance.

I got over it. I've gone back to see the painting over and over; it was still singular, still overpowering, but as a work a team of people once made in a particular time and place. But that first day stayed with me — as a proof that what art does, maybe what it does most completely, is to tell us, make us feel, that what we think we know we don't. There are whole worlds around us that we have never seen. I've always bet on that hunch, but until I left the Frari in Venice it wasn't a conviction, or a faith — and keeping faith with that conviction, or trying to, is why I write.

Dennis Potter wrote the 1981 Steve Martin Depression musical *Pennies from Heaven,* and the indelible BBC-TV musical series *The Singing Detective,* from 1986, and *Lipstick on Your Collar,* from 1993. In these musicals people don't just break into song. Old songs descend on them like visitations, and the original recordings come out of their mouths and change them. The actors are lip-synching, but it feels not as if something is being faked but as if something real, real but never glimpsed before, is being revealed. A dramatic event, but also an idea, is being set loose in the world.

What are the songs? Pop songs from the 1920s into the 1960s. "It's a Sin to Tell a Lie" by Dolly Dawn (out of Jessica Harper's simpering lips). "After You've Gone" by Al Jolson. "Be Bop-a-Lula" by Gene Vincent (Ewan McGregor performs every word in gestures). "Don't Be Cruel" by Elvis Presley. "Ac-Cent-Tchu-Ate the Positive" by Bing Crosby. "Little Bitty Pretty One" by Thurston Harris. "Blues in the Night" by Anne Shelton. The titanic "Pennies from Heaven" by Arthur Tracy (danced by Vernel Bagneris as if there were mouths all over his body). Dozens more. "How do I get that music from way down there bang up front?" Potter said once. "And then I thought, they lip-synch things. I wasn't breaking a mold. I found the ideal way of making these songs real." It was the obvious artifice — sometimes a man's voice coming out of a female character's mouth or vice versa — that let the truth of the songs, and of the characters, feel impossible to refuse. And, coming out of that experience, Potter's manifesto, words I've gone back to again and again since I first encountered them, in an interview Potter did with the film critic Michael Sragow in 1987. "I don't make the mistake that high culture mongers do of assuming that because people like cheap art, their feelings are cheap, too," he said.

> When people say, "Oh, listen, they're playing our song," they don't mean "Our song, this little cheap, tinkling syncopated piece of rubbish is what we felt when we met." What they're saying is, "That song reminds me of the tremendous feeling we had when we met." Some of the songs I use are great anyway, but the cheaper songs are still in the direct line of descent from David's Psalms. They're saying, "Listen, the world isn't quite like this, the world is better than this, there is love in it," "There's you and me in it," or "The sun is shining in it." So-called dumb people, simple people, uneducated people, have as authentic and profound depth of feeling as the most educated on earth.

"And anyone who says different," he said, "is a fascist."

"I think we all have this little theater on top of our shoulders where the past and the present and our aspirations and our memories are simply and inevitably mixed," Potter said that same day in 1987, seven years before he died. "What makes each one of us unique is the potency of the individual mix."

For a moment, in that church in Venice, all of that was in ruins — but that's what art does. That's what it's for — to show you that what you think can be erased, canceled, turned on its head, by something you weren't prepared for. Anything. The turn of a shoulder as an actor delivers a line in a play. The way a guitar passage in a song seems to physically turn over as if it were a person. A scene in a movie when the picture suddenly darkens. A break in a collage that dissolves its apparent language into speaking in tongues. The appearance in an advertisement of something that doesn't belong, that doesn't seem to be selling anything, as if it's the designer's letter in a bottle, a gremlin sneaking in after the piece has been put to bed, a cry for help in a fortune cookie. Those occurrences, those tiny critical events, can generate a transformative power that reaches you far more strongly than it reaches the person next to you, or even anyone else on earth, if it reaches any of them at all. Art produces revelations that you might be unable to explain, or pass on to anyone else — but a revelation that if you are a writer you might try desperately to pass on, in your own words, in your own work.

What is the impulse behind art? "I have to be moved in some way," the guitarist Michael Bloomfield said in 1968, on why he didn't like the San Francisco bands of the time. "They just don't move me enough. The Who moves me, their madness moves me. I like to be moved be it by spectacle, be it by kineticism, be it by some throbbing on 'Papa ooh mau mau' as a chorus, a million times over." And that, he said, was why he played. He was saying, in his way, what I am trying to say: whatever language is the language of your work, if I can move anyone else as that moved me — that "Gimme Shelter," Al Pacino's voice in *The Godfather,* that painting by Titian, moved me from one place to another, from this place on earth to one three steps away, where the world looks not the same — if I can move anyone even a fraction as much as that moved me, if I can spark the same sense of mystery, and awe, and surprise, as that sparked in me, then I'm not wasting my time, or someone else's time. And this is why, in 1947, Albert Camus said, as plainly as Dennis Potter, "There is always a social explanation for what we see in art. Only it doesn't explain anything important."

Most explanations of what we see in art – of what art is, of why people make it, why people pay it any mind, why some art leads to great renown, in other words fame and memory, and some doesn't – are meant to reduce art to something that can be easily translated back into ordinary experience, that can be easily understood – and most explanations of art are meant to exclude a lot of people, and raise up the people who are doing the explaining.

This hit home for me a few years ago, reading a collection of essays about Allen Ginsberg's poem "Howl," first read publicly in 1955, published in 1956 – with almost every one of them about how the poem had changed the writer's life. *This poem changed my life,* one writer after another testified – which is why the word *I* appeared in the first or second sentence of more than half the pieces in the book: I counted. It reminded me of a person who once rushed up to the film critic Manny Farber, one of the crustiest, unsmilingest people you'd ever want to meet, or not want to meet, and said, "Mr. Farber, you changed my life." "I doubt it," he said. *Life is not that facile.*

This poem changed my life, the writers said in chorus. "Can I possibly convey," said one, "how those words" — he was of course talking about the first lines of "Howl," "I saw the best minds of my generation destroyed by madness, starving hysterical naked/dragging themselves through the negro streets at dawn looking for an angry fix" (an early manuscript that Ginsberg sent to Jack Kerouac, on view in the 2016 Paris exhibition *The Beat Generation,* had "angry streets at dawn searching for a negro fix," which says that meaning is a game of chance with rhythm spinning the wheel) — "moved in me, how that cadence undid in a minute's time whatever prior cadences had been voice-tracking my life?" No, he can't. No one could convey anything in writing that impoverishing: "whatever prior cadences," "voice-tracking." But writer after writer is telling you how the poem changed their lives — that is, how it made them writers. Which is a kind of fascist vanity, fascist in the way it erases what the writers are supposedly talking about, replacing the Mona Lisa in her frame with themselves: *If this poem produced a writer like me, it must be good!*

It all comes down to that urge to fascism — the critic's match for a Thatcher-era campaign button, real or from a novel, I can no longer remember:

DO AS YOU'RE TOLD
VOTE CONSERVATIVE

It comes down to the falsity of knowing, as a critic — and all of those "Howl" writers were making arguments about criticism, about how we make sense of what we see, what we hear, and what we think inside and out of the critical events that make up part of a life — what's best for people, to know that some people are of the best and some are worthless, the urge to separate the good from the bad and praise oneself, to decide what books people ought to read, what songs people ought to be moved by, what art they ought to make. People *fight* the experience of art, Pauline Kael wrote in her review of *Bonnie and Clyde,* and so they make a critical response into a set of laws that take away the freedom to respond, rather than try to fashion critical writing that, like art, creates freedom, or reveals the possibility that it exists, or even the fear, as the dadaist Richard Huelsenbeck said at the end of his life, that "liberty really never existed anywhere." It comes down to the notion that, in the end, there is a social explanation for art, which is to say an explanation of what kind of art you should be ashamed of. "At Clarksdale, U.S. Highway 49 intersects Highway 61," David Thomas of

Pere Ubu sang in 2023 in the band's version of the folk song "Worried Man Blues," his voice distant and crinkling, as if it were a transcription from a 1940s radio play. "And that is the crossroads of blues legend. Robert Johnson supposedly sold his soul to the devil. Pablo Picasso never sold his soul to the devil, but a Black guy from the delta, guess that's got to be the explanation." It's the reduction of the mystery in art—where it comes from, where it goes—to the facile explanation of *that poem made me a poet,* that song, that movie, that painting, that piece of writing, that piece of my life, made me a writer, as if why anyone is a writer is something that can be explained at all. All I can do is not to disbelieve in the moments when writing happens, as with one day in 1995, taking a daily walk up the steep Panoramic Way hill behind the football stadium.

I was vaguely thinking about a book I wanted to write, when an opening scene, complete with setting, characters, dialogue, and punchline appeared before me as if on a cue card for a skit I didn't realize I was already playing. I went home, wrote it down, like a stenographer, it seemed—a completely fictional opening about a set of then-obscure Bob Dylan recordings from nearly thirty years before, though when for me criticism reaches its highest pitch the borders between fiction and fact can seem to dissolve.

> In the dressing room in London, the guitarist was looking for a melody. He picked tiny notes off the strings until they fluttered, snapping in the air. The singer turned his head, caught the tune, the title flashing up: sure, "Strange Things Happening Every Day," Sister Rosetta Tharpe, when was it, 1945? Closing in on Tharpe's own guitar line, the guitarist felt for the syncopation in the rhythm, and the song came to life in the singer's mind.

> > On that last great Judgment Day
> > When they drive them all away
> > There are strange things happening
> > every day

> She was shameless, the singer remembered: purer than pure when her mother was alive, backsliding after that. She came onto the Lord's stage in a mink; she had a way with a guitar few men could touch. She was the

black church in the Grand Ole Opry — she'd
even recorded with Pat Boone's father-in-
law, Red Foley, Mr. "Old Shep" himself.
On the other hand, Red Foley had recorded
"Peace in the Valley," hadn't he, the spiri-
tual the Reverend Thomas A. Dorsey had
written as the Second World War began?
The sainted gospel composer, in earlier
days known as Georgia Tom, who'd put his
name on dirty blues? The singer shook his
head: why was he remembering all this? His
memory raced ahead of him. For some rea-
son he remembered that "Strange Things
Happening" had topped the black charts
the same week Hitler killed himself. It was
April 30, 1945; the singer was a month short
of four, Sister Rosetta Tharpe was thirty.
"There's something in the gospel blues,"
she would say years later, "that's so deep
the world can't stand it." Now he heard the
song as if the war had ended yesterday, as if
it were the first time he'd heard it, wherever
that had been — off some road he'd never
remember anything else about, like waking

from a dream you had to get up and live
through.

> If you want to view the climb
> You must learn to quit your lyin'
> There are strange things happening
>   every day

The guitarist was beginning to mumble the
words, faking them, getting only the title
phrase. The singer grinned as he made for
the door. " 'Strange things happening every
day,' " he said. "She got that right."

I didn't write another word for three months. I
wasn't worried — I knew the book was already there,
biding its time.

1. Greil Gerstley

It's like a ghost is writing. Bob Dylan, "Interview with Robert Hilburn," *Los Angeles Times,* April 4, 2004. In *Bob Dylan: The Essential Interviews,* ed. Jonathan Cott (Wenner Books, 2006), 432.

When you put the music with words and things together. Jon Pareles, "Huey Smith, Piano-Pounding Ace of New Orleans R&B, Dies at 89," *New York Times,* February 21, 2023, quoting John Wirt, *Huey "Piano" Smith and the Rockin' Pneumonia Blues* (LSU Press, 2014).

The greatest thing for me. Jason Zinoman, "Richard Belzer Had a Ball with the Relationship Between Comic and Crowd," *New York Times,* February 20, 2023.

Stagger Lee is a free man. GM, *Mystery Train: Images of America in Rock 'n' Roll Music* (1975; Folio Society, 2020), 72.

We think we know what we're doing. Brains, "Money Changes Everything" (Gray Matter, 1978).

If, finally, the conquerors succeed. Albert Camus, *The Rebel: An Essay on Man in Revolt,* trans. Anthony Bower (Vintage Books, 1956), 276.

Shahid watched his lover. Hanif Kureishi, *The Black Album* (Scribner, 1995), 122.

The story he told. Bruce Henderson, *Down to the Sea: An Epic Story of Naval Disaster and Heroism in World War II* (Smithsonian Books, 2007), 181, 183–85, 201, 202.

2. Pauline Kael

In the sixties we believed in a myth. Stanley Booth, *The True Adventures of the Rolling Stones* (1984, 2000; Canongate, 2012), 551.

Criticism is exciting. Pauline Kael, "Circles and Squares" (1963), in *I Lost It at the Movies* (1965; Bantam, 1966), 279.

When Shoeshine *opened in 1947.* Pauline Kael, "*Shoeshine,*" ibid., 102.

I don't care if he is a genius. Pauline Kael, "Some Notes on Chaplin's *Limelight*" (City Lights, 1953), in *Artforum,* March 2002, 123.

The blind girl. James Agee, "Comedy's Greatest Era" (1949), in Agee, *Film Writing and Selected Journalism,* ed. Michael Sragow (Library of America, 2005), 19.

Calvero's gala benefit. Kael, "Some Notes on Chaplin's *Limelight,*" 124.

A lady critic. Andrew Sarris, *The American Cinema: Directors and Directions, 1929–1968* (Dutton, 1968), 26.

Robbe-Grillet. Pauline Kael, "Zeitgeist and Poltergeist" (1964), in *I Lost It at the Movies,* 19.

Sex is the great leveler. Pauline Kael, "*West Side Story,*" ibid., 127.

The delinquent is disturbing. Pauline Kael, "The Glamour of Delinquency" (1955), ibid., 52–53.

Too many people. Pauline Kael, "*Bonnie and Clyde*" (1967), in *Kiss Kiss Bang Bang* (Little, Brown, 1968), 55–56.

There were people trying to stop the show. David Fricke, "Dylan's Dilemma," *Rolling Stone,* December 5, 1985.

Catch the first bullet. Kael, "*Bonnie and Clyde,*" 49.

Bonnie and Clyde *brings.* Ibid., 47.

Once something enters mass culture. Ibid., 63.

There is a story told against Beatty. Ibid., 57.

3. Titian

Let me be strictly honest. Roger Scruton, "A Conversation with Greil Marcus," in *The Way of the Moderns: Six Perspectives on Modernism and Music,* ed. Antoni Pizà (Brepols, 2022), 98.

I don't make the mistake. Dennis Potter quoted in Michael Sragow, "BBC Pro Shows ABC's of Dream Writing," *San Francisco Chronicle,* March 29, 1987.

I have to be moved. Jann Wenner, "Mike Bloomfield" (April 6, 1968), in *The Rolling Stone Interviews* (Paperback Library, 1971), 67–68.

There is always a social explanation. Albert Camus, "What Do You Think of American Literature?" (interview), *Combat* (January 17, 1947), in *Camus at* Combat: *Writing 1944–1947,* ed. Jacqueline Lévi-Valensi, trans. Arthur Goldhammer (Princeton University Press, 2006), 279.

Can I possibly convey. Sven Birkets, "Not Then, Not Now," in *The Poem That Changed America: "Howl" Fifty Years Later,* ed. Jason Schindler (Farrar, Straus & Giroux, 2006), 76.

Liberty really never existed anywhere. Richard Huelsenbeck, "On Leaving America for Good" (1969), in Huelsenbeck, *Memoirs of a Dada Drummer,* ed. Hans J. Kleinschmidt, trans. Joachim Neugroschel (Viking, 1974), 189.

At Clarksdale, U.S. Highway 49. Pere Ubu, "Worried Man Blues," from *Trouble on Big Beat Street* (Cherry Red, 2023).

In the dressing room. GM, *Invisible Republic* (Holt, 1997), 3–4.

My first thanks go to John Donatich of Yale University Press and Michael Kelleher of the Windham-Campbell Literature Prizes, who in the summer of 2022, when the idea of writing anything seemed long in the past, gave me something to point toward: to speak at the 2023 Windham-Campbell writers prizes ceremony on the annual topic of "Why I Write," and to compose a book from which that talk would be drawn. At Yale, I thank as well Abbie Storch, Susan Laity, and so-named copy editor Dan Heaton, but as anyone who has had the privilege of working with him knows, really a friend, counselor, and krill catcher. And Tim Clark, Anne Wagner, and Charles Taylor.

Parts of this book appeared before in very different form. In "Greil Gerstley," I have drawn from a talk I gave for the symposium "Telling Childhood" at the

Richard Hugo House in Seattle in 2006, which was published in 2008 as "Tied to History" in *Threepenny Review*; in ordinary circumstances I would never have spoken about myself, but I knew Dick Hugo and wanted to take part to honor his memory. Parts of "Pauline Kael" appeared in *Artforum* in September 1993 (on *I Lost It at the Movies*) and March 2002 (on her review of *Limelight*). In "Titian," comments on Kirk Varnedoe come from a talk on pop art at Princeton in 2006. I first wrote about my encounter with *The Assumption of the Virgin* in the December 25, 1996, "Artists of the Year" issue of *City Pages* (Minneapolis/St. Paul), and spoke about its effect on my understanding of art in a commencement address at the School of Visual Arts in New York in 2013. There are talismans from all across my writing life that have come up in my work again and again, and many do so here: Camus and *The Rebel*, Dennis Potter on high and low culture, the Rolling Stones' "Gimme Shelter," Stanley Booth on myth, the end of *The Manchurian Candidate,* many more. I've been lucky to share the years with all of them.